A Note to Parents

Frankie I.

DK READERS is a compelling program for beginning readers, designed in conjunction with leading literacy experts, including Dr. Linda Gambrell, Distinguished Professor of Education at Clemson University. Dr. Gambrell has served as President of the National Reading Conference, the College Reading Association, and the International Reading Association.

Beautiful illustrations and superb full-color photographs combine with engaging, easy-to-read stories to offer a fresh approach to each subject in the series. Each DK READER is guaranteed to capture a child's interest while developing his or her reading skills, general knowledge, and love of reading.

The five levels of DK READERS are aimed at different reading abilities, enabling you to choose the books that are exactly right for your child:

Pre-level 1: Learning to read
Level 1: Beginning to read
Level 2: Beginning to read alone
Level 3: Reading alone
Level 4: Proficient readers

The "normal" age at which a child begins to read can be anywhere from three to eight years old. Adult participation through the lower levels is very helpful for providing encouragement, discussing storylines, and sounding out unfamiliar words.

No matter which level you select, you can be sure that you are helping your child learn to read, then read to learn!

DK

LONDON, NEW YORK, MUNICH,
MELBOURNE, AND DELHI

Designer Lisa Robb
Jacket Designer Lauren Rosier
Design Manager Ron Stobbart
Publishing Manager Catherine Saunders
Art Director Lisa Lanzarini
Publishing Director Alex Allan
Pre-Production Producer Andy Hilliard
Producer Louise Daly
Reading Consultant Dr. Linda Gambrell

First published in the United States in 2012
by DK Publishing
375 Hudson Street, New York, New York 10014
10 9 8 7 6 5 4 3 2 1

LEGO and the LEGO Logo are trademarks of The LEGO Group.
Copyright © 2012 The LEGO Group
Produced by Dorling Kindersley
under license from The LEGO Group

Page Design Copyright © 2012 Dorling Kindersley Limited

001—185321—Oct/12

DK books are available at special discounts when purchased in bulk
for sales promotions, premiums, fund-raising, or educational use.
For details, contact:
DK Publishing Special Markets
375 Hudson Street
New York, New York 10014
SpecialSales@dk.com

A catalog record for this book is available
from the Library of Congress.

ISBN: 978-0-7566-9847-8 (Paperback)
ISBN: 978-0-7566-9848-5 (Hardcover)

Color reproduction by Media Development and Printing, UK
Printed and bound in the U.S.A by Lake Book
Manufacturing, Inc.

Discover more at
www.dk.com

www.LEGO.com

Contents

4 The Vampire Awakes!

6 Vampyre Castle

8 Vampyre Bride

9 Zombie Servant

10 Vampyre Hearse

12 Manbats

14 Swamp Creature

16 The Mummy King

18 The Werewolf

20 Ghoulish Graveyard

22 Crazy Scientist's Monster

24 Secret Laboratory

26 The Ghost Train

28 Monster Fighters

30 Daring Heroes

32 Glossary and Index

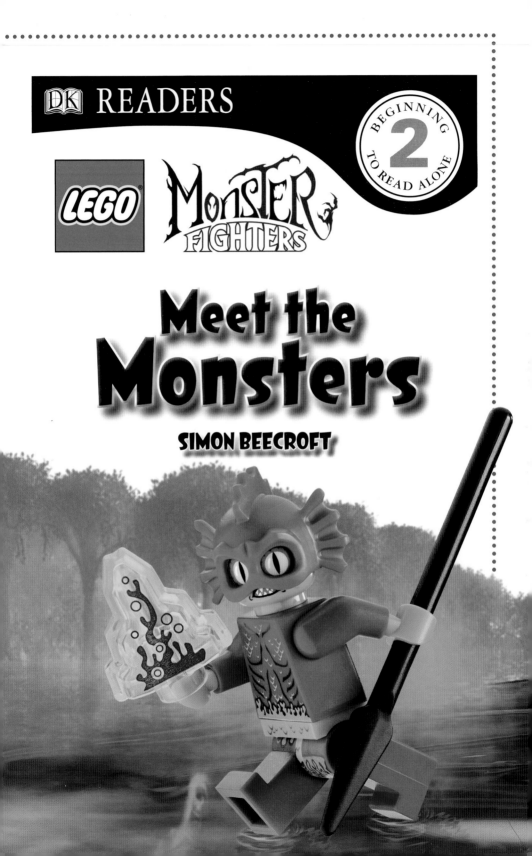

DK READERS

BEGINNING TO READ ALONE
2

LEGO® MONSTER FIGHTERS

Meet the Monsters

SIMON BEECROFT

The Vampire Awakes!

Lord Vampyre has woken
from his centuries-
long sleep.

The time is right to play a little spooky music—and hatch a spooky plot!

Each monster in the Monster World guards a Moonstone, which contains their powers. If Lord Vampyre combines all the Moonstones, he will bring darkness over the world forever!

Magical Moonstones

You can tell which Moonstone belongs to which monster by its symbol: An Ancient Egyptian evil eye for the Mummy and a howling wolf for the Werewolf!

Vampyre Castle

Lord Vampyre is the leader of all the monsters. He lives in the darkest, blackest castle in the Monster World.

Bat statue

Deadly Machine

Lord Vampyre has constructed a Moonstone machine at the top of the tallest tower. When six Moonstones are placed within the machine, the Moon will block out the Sun forever!

Lord Vampyre's coffin lies inside the castle's dungeon—his resting place for many centuries.

It is very dangerous to enter this creepy castle. Strange creatures are hiding in the shadows. And watch out for hidden trapdoors and pop-out spikes. You have been warned!

Vampyre Bride

Count Vampyre's fanged bride is
the love of his life—after
Moonstones, that is!
She mixes enchanted
potions and is always
reminding her
husband to be as
evil as possible.

Enchanted
frogs and
toadstools

Zombie Servant

Renfield is Count
Vampyre's
faithful
zombie
servant.
He drives Count
Vampyre's car and
obeys his every
order. Watch
out for this
ghoulish driver,
though. Renfield has a temper!

Vampyre Hearse

Lord Vampyre's hearse is no
ordinary funeral car. It can race
at top speeds! Lord Vampyre's
coffin slides inside. The sneaky
villain can pop up through
the roof to give
people the fright
of their lives!

Lord Vampyre's Moonstone sits
on the front
of the car.

Boo!
Scared you!

Manbats

Two manbats live in Count
Vampyre's castle. They are half-
man, half-bat, with piercing red
eyes and sharp fangs.

Batwing

Blood-sucking
fangs

The manbats scare
away intruders. During
the day, they hang upside
down from the towers and sleep.
The Manbats are also good
spies. Their large, sensitive ears
can hear everything. If there are
intruders—it's straight to the
dungeon for them!

Swamp Creature

Strange creatures live in every corner of the Monster World. Would you like to meet them and learn their secrets?

Spiky head crest

Spear for poking minifigures

In the marshlands, a Swamp Creature guards a glowing green Moonstone. This ghastly ghoul is part-fish, part-reptile, with yellow eyes and sharp teeth. The Creature commands the waters of the swamp and can create huge waves!

Swamp Secrets
Strange slimy things live in the murky waters of the swamp, from biting fish to poisonous frogs. Watch where you put your feet!

The Mummy King

The Mummy King rides a ghostly chariot through the bad lands of the Monster World. When he comes upon any hopeless travelers, he puts a curse on them.

Scorpion clasp

The Mummy King's skeleton horse carries a powerful purple Moonstone on his back—in a scorpion clasp. Eerie!

Don't stare into his eyes!

The Werewolf

The ferocious Werewolf prowls and howls in the deepest forest of the Monster Realm. His fangs and claws are razor-sharp! The Werewolf hides in a secret catapult hidden in a treetop.

Then he springs out right on top of unwary visitors! *Howwwwl!*

Secret Lair
The Werewolf hides his orange Moonstone in his lair beneath a huge, twisted tree.

Ghoulish Graveyard

This graveyard is covered with green fog. The air is filled with strange moans and groans. And now there's a loud creaking noise.

Oh no! Those old graves are opening up by themselves— it's the Zombie Groom with his beautiful Bride, and their Zombie Driver!

The Undead
The Zombies are very angry and want to bite you to turn you into a Zombie. They think you want to steal their precious Moonstone!

Crazy Scientist's Monster

Strange experiments are taking place in a secret laboratory. The Crazy Scientist is mixing explosive chemicals and playing with the power of lightning. Now look at what he has created. A monster stitched together from bits of bodies!

Green
Moonstone

The
Crazy
Scientist's
Monster is
unnaturally
strong. He will
attack anyone
who tries to
steal his
master's
powerful green Moonstone.

Secret Laboratory

The Crazy Scientist used the power of lightning to bring his Monster to life in his laboratory. He placed his Moonstone on a tall tower to attract the lightning. CRASH! The creature wakes!

All around the laboratory are glowing rats and spiders, scary potions, skulls... and a prison cell, where YOU might end up if you're not careful!

The Ghost Train

What's that noise? Is it choo-choo—or wooh-wooh? Because this eerie Ghost Train is haunted by wailing, glowing ghosts.

Ghost train
When the Ghost Train moves, its bat wings flap up and down in a horrifying manner! The front of the train is a ghostly, glowing face.

These white-sheeted ghouls guard a shining blue Moonstone.

The spooky Ghost Train flies across the wild, misty moors. On a dark, moonlit night, when the Ghost Train's glowing, green face is speeding towards you... You'd better run for your life!

Prison wagon

Monster Fighters

With all these monsters about, the world must surely be doomed! Or is it? A team of brave Monster Fighters are determined to stop Lord Vampyre. The leader, Dr. Rodney Rathbone, carries a fencing sword and has a robotic leg!

His side-kick, Jack McHammer, is strong and tough. He lost his right arm in a monster fight and now has a robotic replacement.

Jack is armed with a monster-bashing hammer.

Daring Heroes

Three more daring heroes join the gang of Monster Fighters. Frank Rock is a rebel on a mission to mash monsters. Ann Lee is an expert crossbow fighter. (She even keeps a spare arrow in her hair!) Quinton Steele is a big game hunter who wears the fangs of a dead werewolf on his belt.

These Monster Fighters are daring heroes, all right. But who will prevail and claim the powerful Moonstones?

Glossary

Crossbow
a wooden bow that shoots short arrows

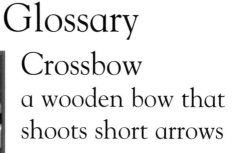

Fencing sword
a thin sword with a little round button at the tip

Mummy
a dead body preserved inside bandages

Vampire
a corpse that rises from its grave to drink blood

Zombie
A mindless walking dead person